CAROLS

JOY TO THE WORLD!

Fifteen sacred carols and
Christmas hymns for mixed voices

EDITED AND ARRANGED
BY JOHN RUTTER

MUSIC DEPARTMENT

OXFORD

UNIVERSITY PRESS

PREFACE

JOY TO THE WORLD! presents fifteen of the finest and best-loved sacred carols and Christmas hymns in choral arrangements which may be performed either separately, or else as a sequence (with or without readings and prayers) forming a complete Christmas service or concert.

Each arrangement is complete in itself, so the suggested sequence (shown with readings and prayers on p. 58) can be shortened or altered to suit the needs of different choirs and occasions.

Five Christmas hymns are included, in arrangements for choir, congregation/audience, and organ or orchestra. The opening hymn, *O come all ye faithful,* is preceded by an optional fanfare for brass, percussion, and organ. In addition, *Joy To The World* is presented in a special extended arrangement for choir. Six carols are arranged for unaccompanied choir, and three for choir with piano, organ, or orchestra.

Instrumentation for the accompanied items is listed at the foot of their first pages. The hymns are scored for full orchestra, but any of the woodwind, brass and percussion may be omitted if organ is available. The carols are scored for small orchestra, or less. All the accompaniments may satisfactorily be played by piano or organ alone.

Companion volumes of the John Rutter Carols:

O HOLY NIGHT (thirteen sacred carols and Christmas hymns)
WE WISH YOU A MERRY CHRISTMAS (twelve secular carols and Christmas songs)

Note:
Orchestral scores and parts are available from Oxford University Press.

CONTENTS

Carols suitable for unaccompanied singing are marked thus: *

TITLE	PAGE
O come, all ye faithful.	1
J.F. Wade arr. John Rutter	
*Lo, how a rose e'er blooming	7
Old German arr. M. Praetorius	
*'Twas in the moon of winter time	8
Canadian trad. arr. John Rutter	
Joy to the world!	13
Lowell Mason arr. John Rutter	
It came upon the midnight clear	20
R.S. Willis arr. John Rutter	
*Away in a manger	22
W.J. Kirkpatrick arr. John Rutter	
*Silent night	24
Franz Grüber arr. John Rutter	
O little town of Bethlehem	28
Lewis Redner arr. John Rutter	
*Rise up, shepherd, and follow	30
Spiritual arr. John Rutter	
*In dulci jubilo	33
German 14th -cent. arr. B. Gesius	
How great our joy!	34
German trad. arr. John Rutter	
While shepherds watched their flocks	38
Handel arr. John Rutter	
Three kings of Orient	40
J.H. Hopkins arr. John Rutter	
Bring a torch, Jeannette, Isabella.	47
(Un flambeau, Jeannette, Isabelle)	
French trad. arr. John Rutter	
God rest you merry, gentlemen.	54
English trad. arr. John Rutter	
A service of readings and carols.	58

O COME, ALL YE FAITHFUL
(Adeste fideles)

for Mixed Voices, S. A. T. B., Opt. Choir or Congregation
with Organ*

Words tr.
F. OAKELEY, W. T. BROOKE
and others

J. F. WADE (?)
arranged by JOHN RUTTER
(verses 6 and 7)

3. See how the shepherds,
   Summoned to his cradle,
   Leaving their flocks, draw nigh with lowly fear;
   We too will thither
   Bend our joyful footsteps:
       O come, etc.

4. Lo! star - led chieftains,
   Magi, Christ adoring,
   Offer him incense, gold, and myrrh;
   We to the Christ Child
   Bring our hearts' oblations:
       O come, etc.

5. Child, for us sinners
   Poor and in the manger,
   Fain we embrace thee, with awe and love;
   Who would not love thee,
   Loving us so dearly?
       O come, etc.

To next page for verse 6

Instrumentation: 2Fl, 2Ob, 2Cl, Bsn, 2Hn, 3Tpt, 2Tbn, B.Tbn, Tba, Timp, Perc, Organ, Strings. Woodwind, brass and percussion are optional if organ is available. This arrangement is preceded by an optional fanfare for 2Hn, 3Tpt, 2Tbn, B. Tbn, Tba, Timp, Perc, Organ (optional). Score and parts are included with the orchestral rental material for the hymn. Orchestral scores and parts are available on rental.

2

To the next page for verse 7

4

6

LO, HOW A ROSE E'ER BLOOMING

Original German text, 16th century
Tr. THEODORE BAKER

Old German Tune
arranged by
M. PRAETORIUS (1571-1621)

* Soprano and Tenor may exchange parts in verse 2 to good effect. Verse 1 may be repeated after verse 2.

'TWAS IN THE MOON OF WINTER TIME

for Mixed Voices, S. A. T. B., *a cappella*

Words by
JEAN DE BRÉBEUF (1593–1649)
Tr. J. E. Middleton

Canadian traditional tune
arranged by
JOHN RUTTER

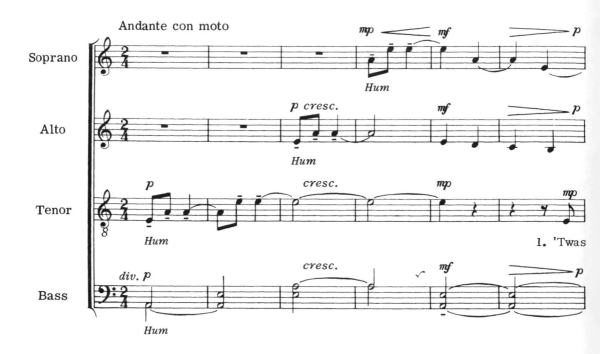

in the moon of win-ter time, When all the birds had fled, That

migh-ty Git-chi Man-i-tou Sent an-gel choirs in-stead; Be-

-fore their light the stars grew dim, And won-d'ring hun-ters heard the hymn:___
unis.

mp   cresc.

Je - sus your King is born, Je - sus is born, In ex-cel-sis
mp
(Hum)

mp   cresc.

Je - sus your King is born, Je - sus is born, In ex-cel-sis
mp
(Hum)

10

JOY TO THE WORLD!
(extended arrangement)
for Mixed Voices, S. A. T. B., with Keyboard*

Words by
ISAAC WATTS

Melody by LOWELL MASON (1792-1872)
(based on HANDEL)
arranged by JOHN RUTTER

1. Joy to the world! the Lord is come: Let
4. He rules the world with truth and grace, And

earth re-ceive her King; Let
makes the na - tions prove The

* Instrumentation: 2Ob, Bsn, 2Tpt, Timp, Organ or Harpsichord, Strings. Orchestral scores and parts are available on rental.
A simple harmonization of this hymn, suitable for unaccompanied or congregational use, is included in the companion volume, **O HOLY NIGHT**.

ev - 'ry_ heart _____ pre - pare him_ room, _____ And
glo - ries_ of _____ his right - eous - ness, _____ And

heav'n and na - ture_sing, And_ heav'n and na - ture_sing, And_
won - ders of his_love, And_ won-ders of his_love, And_

And heav'n and na - ture sing, And heav'n and na - ture
And won - ders of his love, And won - ders of his

after v.4: to CODA (p.19)

heav'n, _____ and_ heav'n _____ and na - ture sing.
won - ders,_ won - ders of his love.

sing, _____ and heav'n and na - ture sing.
love, _____ and won - ders of _____ his love.

after v.4: to CODA (p.19)

A
2. Joy to the earth! the Sa - vior reigns:
Let

men their songs em - ploy;
While

far as the curse is found.

far as the curse is found.

far as the curse is found.

far as the curse is found.

D.S. for Verse 4
(back to p.13)

Coda (from p. 14)

D.S. for Verse 4
(back to p.13)

Coda (from p. 14)

IT CAME UPON THE MIDNIGHT CLEAR

Words by
E. H. SEARS

R. S. WILLIS (1819-1900)
Descant by JOHN RUTTER

Instrumentation: 2Fl, 2Ob, 2Cl, Bsn, 2Hn, 2Tpt, 2Tbn, B.Tbn, Tba, Timp, Strings. Woodwind, brass and percussion are optional if organ is available. Orchestral scores and parts are available on rental.

gold; When peace ov - er all the earth Its

gold: _____ 'Peace on the earth, good - will to men, From
world; _____ A - bove its sad and low - ly plains They
wrong; _____ And man, at war with man, hears not The
gold; _____ When peace shall ov - er all the earth Its

an - cient splen - dours fling, The world send back,

heav'n's all - gra - cious King! _____ The world in so - lemn
bend on ho - v'ring wing; _____ And ev - er o'er its
love - song which they bring: _____ O hush the noise, ye
an - cient splen - dours fling, _____ And the whole world send

send back the song the an - gels sing. _____

still - ness lay To hear the an - gels sing. _____
Ba - bel sounds The bless - ed an - gels sing. _____
men of strife, And hear the an - gels sing! _____
back the song Which now the an - gels sing. _____

AWAY IN A MANGER
(Original tune)*
for Mixed Voices, S. A. T. B., a cappella

Words anon.

Melody by
W. I. KIRKPATRICK (1838-1921)
arranged by JOHN RUTTER

*An accompanied arrangement of the setting of this text by J. R. Murray is included in the companion volume, O HOLY NIGHT.

Hum

mp unis.

2. The cat-tle are_ low-ing, the_ ba-by a - wakes, But_

lit - tle Lord Je - sus no_ cry-ing he makes. I

love thee, Lord_ Je - sus! Look_ down from the sky, And_

D. C. for verse 3

stay by my side un - til_ morn - ing is nigh.

SILENT NIGHT

for Mixed Voices, S. A. T. B., *a cappella*

German Words by
JOSEF MOHR
Tr. J. F. YOUNG

FRANZ GRÜBER
arranged by
JOHN RUTTER

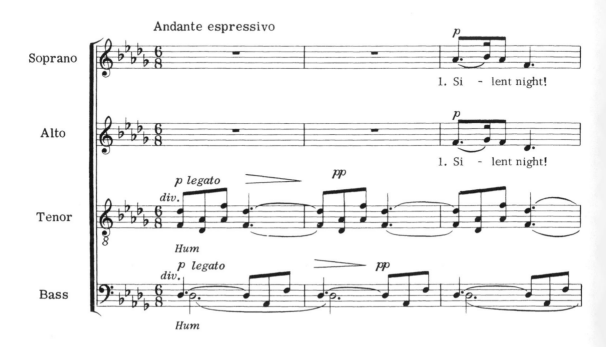

O LITTLE TOWN OF BETHLEHEM

Words by
PHILLIPS BROOKS

LEWIS REDNER (1831-1908)
Descant by JOHN RUTTER

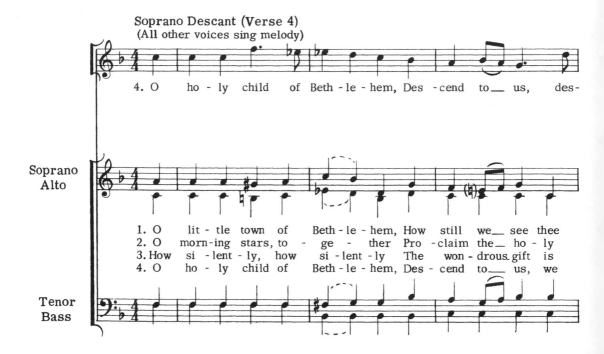

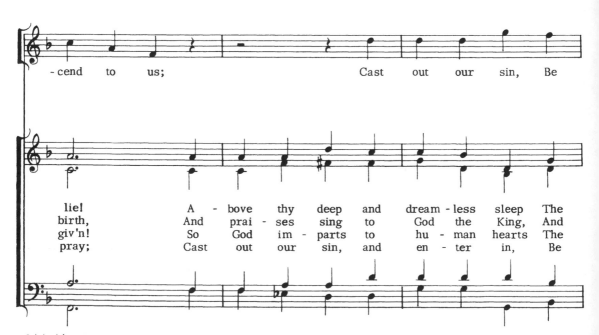

Original key G. Alto and tenor parts in the penultimate measure adapted.

Instrumentation: 2Fl, 2Ob, 2Cl, Bsn, 2Hn, 2Tpt, 2Tbn, B. Tbn, Tba, Timp, Strings. Woodwind, brass and timp are optional if organ is available. Orchestral scores and parts are available on rental.

RISE UP, SHEPHERD, AND FOLLOW

for Mixed Voices, S. A. T. B., *a cappella*

Spiritual
arranged by
JOHN RUTTER

31

IN DULCI JUBILO

Original text 14th century
Tr. R. L. PEARSALL*

German, 14th century
Arranged by
B. GESIUS (1601)

(Con moto)

Soprano
Alto

1. In dul - ci ju - bi - lo _____ Let us our hom - age
2. O Je - su par - vu - le! _____ I yearn for thee al -
3. O Pa - tris ca - ri - tas, _____ O Na - ti le - ni -
4. U - bi sunt gau - di - a, _____ If that they be not

Tenor
Bass

shew; _____ Our heart's joy re - cli - neth In prae - se - pi -
- way! _____ Hear me, I be - seech _____ thee, O Puer op - ti -
- tas! _____ Deep - ly were we stain - èd Per nos - tra cri - mi -
there? _____ There are an - gels sing - ing No - va can - ti -

- o _____ And like a bright star shi - neth Ma - tris in gre - mi -
- me! _____ My pray - er let it reach thee, O Prin - ceps glo - ri -
- na; _____ But thou hast for us gain - èd Coe - lo - rum gau - di -
- ca, _____ And there the bells are ring - ing In Re - gis cu - ri -

- o. _____ Al - pha es et O, _____ Al - pha es _____ et O.
- ae! _____ Tra - he me post te! _____ Tra - he me _____ post te!
- a. _____ O that we were there! _____ O that we _____ were there!
- a: _____ O that we were there! _____ O that we _____ were there!

* The text given here is a translation of the one originally written for the melody. An accompanied arrangement of the same melody to the text *Good Christian men, rejoice* is included in the companion volume, **O HOLY NIGHT.**

HOW GREAT OUR JOY!

for Mixed Voices, S. A. T. B., with Organ*

German traditional carol
arranged by JOHN RUTTER

* Instrumentation: 2Fl/Picc, 2Ob, 2Cl, Bsn, 2Hn, Perc, Strings.
Orchestral scores and parts are available on rental.

V. 1: All Voices
V. 2: All Voices

1st time

f

Praise we the Lord in heav'n on high!

1st time

2nd time

*Choir 1   *p dolce e legato*

3. There shall the Child lie in a stall,

*Choir 2   *pp legato*

Hum

pp legato

2nd time

cresc.   *mf*

This Child who shall re-deem us all. How great our joy!

cresc.   *mp*

How great our joy!

How great our joy! __

cresc.   *mp*

✱ If preferred, Choir 1 part may be sung by a solo voice
and Choir 2 part by the full choir.

WHILE SHEPHERDS WATCHED THEIR FLOCKS

for Mixed Voices, S. A. T. B., with Organ*

Words by NAHUM TATE

G. F. HANDEL
Verse 6 arranged by
JOHN RUTTER

3. 'To you in David's town this day
Is born of David's line
A Saviour, who is Christ the Lord;
And this shall be the sign:

4. 'The heavenly Babe you there shall find
To human view displayed,
All meanly wrapped in swathing bands,
And in a manger laid.'

5. Thus spake the Seraph; and forthwith
Appeared a shining throng
Of angels praising God, who thus
Addressed their joyful song:

* Instrumentation: 2Fl, 2Ob, 2Cl, Bsn, 2Hn, 2Tpt, 2Tbn, B.Tbn, Tba, Timp, Strings. Woodwind, brass and timp are optional if organ is available. Orchestral scores and parts are available on rental.

THREE KINGS OF ORIENT
(accompanied version)
for Mixed Voices, S. A. T. B., with Keyboard*

Words and Music by
J. H. HOPKINS
arranged by JOHN RUTTER

*Instrumentation: 2Fl, 2Ob, 2Cl, 2Bsn, 2Hn, Perc, Hp, Strings. Orchestral scores and parts are available on rental.
An unaccompanied arrangement of this carol is included in the companion volume, **O HOLY NIGHT**.

B Verses 2 and 3

Guide us to thy per - fect light.

B Verses 2 and 3

V. 2: Tenor Solo or Semi-Chorus
V. 3: Baritone Solo or Semi-Chorus

2. Born a king on Beth-le-hem plain, Gold I bring to crown him a-gain,
3. Frank-in-cense to of-fer have I, In-cense owns a De-i-ty nigh,

Pno.

S.
A.

p 2. Hum
mp 3. Aw

T.
B.

Pno.

cresc.   f   dim.   Refrain D. S.
                                                   (back to p. 41)

King for ev - er, Ceas-ing nev - er, O - ver us all to reign:
Prayer and prais - ing, All men rais - ing, Wor-ship him, God most high:

cresc.   dim.

cresc.   dim.

BRING A TORCH, JEANNETTE, ISABELLA

(Un flambeau, Jeannette, Isabelle)

for Mixed Voices, S. A. T. B., with Piano*

English tr. by
E. C. NUNN

French traditional carol
arranged by JOHN RUTTER

Quite relaxed; a gentle one-in-the-bar ($\downarrow \cdot = 60$)

Piano

mf
Bsns.
Obs.
Drum
etc.

S.A.

Sopranos and Altos
unis. mf

1. Bring a torch, _ Jean -
1. *Un flam - beau, _ Jean -*

T.B.

Fls.

Obs.

-nette, Is - a - bel - la! Bring a torch, to the cra - dle run!
-nette, Is - a - bel - le, Un flam - beau, _ cou - rons au ber - ceau!

* Instrumentation: 2Fl, 2Ob, 2Bsn, Perc, Strings (optional). Orchestral scores and parts are available.

Moth - er! Ah! __ ah! beau-ti - ful is her Son.
bel - le, Ah! __ ah! __ que l'En-fant est beau!

Moth - er! Ah! ah! beau-ti - ful is her Son.
bel - le, Ah! ah! ah! que l'En-fant est beau!

Hum

Tacet to D

Soprano Solo or Semi-Chorus
mp dolce espress.

2. It is wrong when the Child__ is sleep-ing, It is wrong__ to
2. C'est un tort quand l'En-fant __ som-meil - le, C'est un tort de cri-

S.

A.

T.

B.

Hush! see — how fast he sleeps! ____
chut! chut! voy -ez comme il dort! ____

Hush! ____ how he sleeps! ____
chut! ____ comme il dort! ____

Hush! ____ Hush! ____ Hush! ____ he sleeps! ____
chut! ____ chut! ____ chut! ____ il dort! ____

Obs.

p

Fls.

p

3. Soft - ly to ___ the lit - tle sta - ble, Soft - ly for ___ a mo - ment
3. *Dou - ce - ment dans l'é - ta - ble clo - se, Dou - ce - ment, ve - nez un mo -*

p

GOD REST YOU MERRY, GENTLEMEN

for Mixed Voices, S. A. T. B., Congregation, with Organ*

English traditional carol
arranged by
JOHN RUTTER

1. God rest you merry, gen-tle-men, Let no-thing you dis-may, For Je-sus Christ our Sa-vior Was born up-on this day, To save us all from Sa-tan's power When we were gone a-stray: O— ti-dings of com-fort and joy, com-fort and joy, O— ti-dings of com-fort and joy.

3. The shep-herds at those ti-dings Re-joic-èd much in mind, And left their flocks a-feed-ing, In tem-pest, storm and wind, And went to Beth-le-hem straight-way This bless-ed babe to find:

Verses 1 and 3
Choir and Congregation

* Instrumentation: 2Fl, 2Ob, 2Cl, Bsn, 2Hn, 2Tpt, 2Tbn, B. Tbn, Tba, Timp, Perc, Strings. Woodwind, brass and percussion are optional if organ is available. Orchestral scores and parts are available on rental.

* originally: *All others doth deface*

A SERVICE OF READINGS AND CAROLS

OPENING HYMN *O come, all ye faithful*

BIDDING PRAYER *(spoken by the Minister)*

Beloved in Christ, be it at this Christmas-tide our care and delight to hear again the message of the angels, and in heart and mind to go even unto Bethlehem and see this thing which is come to pass, and the Babe lying in a manger.

Therefore let us read and mark in Holy Scripture the tale of the loving purposes of God and the glorious redemption brought us by this Holy Child.

But first, let us pray for the needs of the whole world; for peace on earth and goodwill among all his people; for unity and brotherhood within the Church he came to build, and especially in this our congregation.

And because this would rejoice his heart, let us remember, in his name, the poor and helpless, the cold, the hungry, and the oppressed; the sick and them that mourn, the lonely and the unloved, the aged and the little children; all those who know not the Lord Jesus, or who love him not, or who by sin have grieved his heart of love.

Lastly, let us remember before God all those who rejoice with us, but upon another shore, and in a greater light, that multitude which no man can number, whose hope was in the Word made flesh, and with whom in this Lord Jesus we for evermore are one.

These prayers and praises let us humbly offer up to the throne of heaven, in the words which Christ himself hath taught us:

THE LORD'S PRAYER *(spoken by all)*

CAROLS *Lo, how a rose e'er blooming*
        'Twas in the moon of winter time
        Joy to the world!

HYMN *It came upon the midnight clear*

READING   St Luke 2, vv. 1-7

CAROLS *Away in a manger*
        Silent night

HYMN *O little town of Bethlehem*

READING St Luke 2, vv. 8-16

CAROLS *Rise up, shepherd, and follow*
        In dulci jubilo
        How great our joy!

HYMN *While shepherds watched their flocks*

READING   St Matthew 2, vv. 1-11

CAROLS *Three kings of Orient*
        Bring a torch, Jeannette, Isabella

READING   Isaiah 60, vv. 1-6, 19 (*or* St John 1, vv. 1-14)

> *Minister* The Lord be with you
> *Congregation* And with thy spirit
> *Minister* Let us pray

THE COLLECT FOR CHRISTMAS EVE *(spoken by the Minister)*

O God, who makes us glad with the yearly remembrance of the birth of thy only Son, Jesus Christ: Grant that as we joyfully receive him for our Redeemer, so we may with sure confidence behold him, when he shall come to be our judge; who liveth and reigneth with thee and the Holy Spirit, one God, world without end. *Amen.*

THE BLESSING *(spoken by the Minister)*

May he who by his Incarnation gathered into one things earthly and heavenly, fill you with the sweetness of inward peace and goodwill; and the blessing of God Almighty, the Father, the Son, and the Holy Spirit, be upon you and remain with you always. *Amen.*

CLOSING HYMN *God rest you merry, gentlemen*